MY HERITAGE

BY

LASAN
SENI
DARBOE

My Heritage
Copyright © Lasan Seni Darboe 2011

ISBN 13 Digit 978-0-9749682-3-0
ISBN 10 Digit 0-9749682-3-4

Library of Congress Control Number: 2011907368

Illustrated by Robert P. Lozano
Design Consultant by Sr. Margaret McKenna,RSHM
Edited by Andria Marcus
First Published 2011
ScorpionPublishing.com
Scorpionbooks@yahoo.com
Limited Edition

MY HERITAGE
Poetry

BY LASAN SENI DARBOE

Illustrated by Roberto P. Lozano

Scorpion Publishing
Scorpionbooks@yahoo.com

MY HERITAGE
ACKNOWLEDGEMENTS

I dedicate this book to all my colorful friends and family.
Especially all the people I had the great joy of coaching, and most importantly
how much they taught me.

Anderson (Jazmyn, Kent, LaDonna) Aspell (Jenny, Ken, Kati, Lauren) Bartman (Barbara, Liza)
Bell (Melvin, Valerie, Jared) Bello (Afusatu, Fausat, Habeeb, Wasin, Alhaja Akanni)
Berger (Lenny, Melissa, Gaby) Charlston (Jeff, Donna, Gavin, Trevor)
Brooks (Randy, Cameron, Brandon) Cale (Chuck, Jessie, Whitney, Walter, Betsy)
Ceesay (Ben, Jorjo, Jula, Kudo) Chodosh (Josh, Perrin, Max, Anya, Lydia) Katherine Calvert,
Conway (Tony, Nancy, Sean) Cummings (Neil, Ronnie, Julia) Coleman (Dan, Donna, Tyler)
Dardick (Larry, Alex, Kate Naples)Washington (Tom, Cassandra, Courtney, Cameron, Channing)
Darboe (Mustapha, Sankung, Fatoumatta, Yahaddy, Karim, Satang, Seni, Musa, Jatou)
Dillingham (Del, Gail, Kerry, Christopher) Drummond (Wylie, Catherine, Cristen, Wylie)
Dubbins (Margie, Bob, Jackie, Andrew) Farb (Scott, Joanie, Harry, Bess Lurie)
Feldman (Gerald, Gloria, Mark, Nicole, Mindy) Flores (Stacy, Cindy) Sara & Joey Kramer,
Floegel-Shetty (Vivek, Christina, Astrid, Rohan, Lara) Sarah & Katherine Brunner,
Goldman (David, Myra, Sam, Sooky, Max, Zach, Seth, Jessie, Eli, Jonah, Jory)
Gordon (Johnny, Carol, Ryan, Shaun) Huron (Jeffery, Raquel, Erica, Ethan, Alexis)
Hiedewohl (Lovorka, Andre, Marie, Laurel) Gables (Rick, Christina, Sharon) Flynn Coleman,
Heintz (John, Maureen, Kelly, Molly, Will, Jack) Ivory (Roosevelt, Wendy, Kai, Kalle, Kristaan)
Kayne (Ric, Susanne, Jennie, Maggie, Saree) Kornfield (Sharon, Randy, James, Colin)
Lazor (Patty, Joseph, Kelly, Molly) Lake (Gilbert, Gwen, Brandon) Orlando (Gigi & Emmanuel)
Locher (William, Cynthia, Alyson, Stephanie, Lauren) Gordon (Marty, Justin, Jessica)
Matthews (Kim, Jill, Sasha, Channel, K.C, Jayden, Trudy) Ayers (Jim, Paula, Alex)
Mardirossian (Garo, Kathy, Ani, Nora, Kevin) Martin (Wayne, Germaine, Chris, Evan, Ariel)
Mczka (Michael, Elaine, Katherine, Elizabeth) Migliazzo (Larry, Patricia, Connie, Kelly)
Milam (Edwin, Rebecca, Sarah, Meghan, Mara) Mortimer (Keith, Dana, Ryan, Sammy)
Watne (Kevin, Ann, India, Frances, Holden, Reed) Lobodzinski (Maria, Richard, Vivien, Cora)
Olson (Roger, Lisa, Jessica, Dana) Pop (Jeff, Belinda, Sammy, Alex, Jackie) Eugene Damiani,
Pellikka (Edwina, Tamora Phil, Max) Perez (Ernesto, Celestina, Maritza) Jeremy Lake,
Robertson (Pam, Brittany) Romero (Fernando, Kaye, Eric) Spinner (Greg, Carol, Juliette)
Stitzel (Don, Elba, Vivian) Sullivan (Brian, Mary, Molly, Megan) Chuck & Joyce Kim,
Revich (Ira, Barbara, Recbecca, Matthew) Rosso (John, Connie, Julie, Kristine)
Ryan (Christine, Jennifer, Shannon) Salvaryn (Jan, Amanda, Deanna, Lauren) Phillip Harr,
Sibthorpe (Stephen, Anna, Annabelle) Sophia Khan, Sinnott (Bob, Carey) Scott & Joshua Barth
Taylor (Macgruder, Eleanora, Macgruder, Totiyanna, Brian) Treibatch (Igal, Daniel)
TimoTeo (Mu, Veronica, Leana, Renee Kyla, Aliah) Towle (Ed, Joan, Allyson, Daryn, Mia)
Vangsness (Kristen, Tom, CT, Kella, Erica, James) Virgo (Paul, Linda, Asa, Jodee)
Williams (Reggie, Pam, Christopher, Cameroon) Willson (Perry, Sharon, Tracy, Ashley)
Otto Stallworth Sr & Jr, Winegred (Michael, Justin) Bernet (Kevin, Lori, Nicole, Bradley)
Wong (David, Kathy, Matthew) Wormser (Ron, Florence, Camille, Vanessa) Flavio Ribeiro
Wrenn (Susan, Dylan, Ruby) Youngblood (Julie, Jordie) Zarider (David, Barbara, Evan, Matt)
Dylan & Maddy McCarthy, Washburn (Catherine, Elizabeth) Zimmerman (Mara, Hannah)
Wilson (Wayne, Jan, Kate) Gregory & Jade Sherman, Terry & Alex Mitchell, Igor Spigelman
Emily, Alison Litvak, (Steve, Evan Morris) Markus, Alexis Silbiger. Joe & Stephanie Johnson
Xóchitl Green, Zoe Henry, Kristyna & Mandy Preciado, Riley Newkirk, Tatiana Estrada,
Kendall Ferguson, Natalie Aguilar, Viviana Yapanqui, Chase Cunningham, Marissa Williams,
Dominique Marciano, Taymar Cox, Sophia Russo, Darielle Preston, Michall Singleton,
Angelina Moreno, Cecilia & Isaiah Coronado, Breena Berck, Kristen Ortega, Maya Grey,
Duncan Bochicchio, Gordon Bylsma, Quinn Brodey, Joseph Corrigan, Ryan Feinberg,
Patrick King, Gefen Laredo, Johnny Leiter, Etienne Leroux, Blake Nosratian, Steven Suhun,
Alex Oberfeld, Issa O'Dell, Eli Putman, Daniel Scheir, Alan Sneider, Antoine Van Lier,
Sam Wolk, Anders Uhrenholdt, Chasen Washington, Jackson Wildasin, Casey Weaver,
Devin Burstein, Kaysan Ghasseeminejad, Golan Corshidi, Caleb Paydar, Leeran Shlomo,
Ricardo Lopez, Daniel Khalfin, Nathan Daneshgar, Leah Bonilla, Yasmine Tabatabai,
Charlotte Toates, Rachel Rodriguez, Salina Mclellan, Nicole Sharf, Ivonne Pur, Rachel Wallis
Rachel Kove, Jessie Kavanaugh, Amanda Brandeis, Sara Safran, Marie Hopkins, Tanya Djafar
Christina Butler, Veronica Bouza, Claire Dorfman, Camille Edwards, Rebecca Friedland,
Acacia Friedman, Julia Gautreaux, Itchel Guzman, Kaitlyn Hafdell, Miranda Landfield,
Jennifer Mair, Shannon & Kellie Mossler, Jocelyn Karlan, Christina Phillips, Ashley Menzis,
Elaine Choi, Gina Hendron, Mark & Joanna Korshak, Adrien Bishlawy, Billy Kaplan,
Frankie Pfister, Kevin Seto, David Marenberg, Nathan Reed, Jon Blumenfeld, Nicholas Stone,
Ryan Franks, Chukwuma Ekwueme, Chris Habu, Roberto Calogera, Tom Lesniewski,
Jozeta, Katja McKiernan, Adelaide Seaman, Katie Lee, Kelsey Sherman, Mahlke Michelle,
Lauren Argano, Tiffany Azad, Adeline Black, Kara Duncan

Amine & Kathleen Harris, April Kacena, Emma Loos, Nicole McMahan, Sarah Nuslein,
Meagan Rafferty, Callie Rehm, Julia Robinson, Alex Rodberg, Lily Royer, Mina Bahadori,
Claire Fitzgerald,, Justine Talay, Amanda Valencia, Natasha Wachtel, Alexandria Wierzba
Morgan Alessini, Michelle Folan, Loren Hart, Sofia John, Lillian Moriarty, Jessica Turkmany,
Ashley Chavez, Stephanie Darling, Cassie Hoppic, Madeline Whitesell, Alison McCandless,
Megan McCann, Ragnhildur Veigarsdottir, Ashley Paillet, Morgan Thomas, Anaisy Tolentino,
Jade Byrd, Caitlin & Kaleigh Homstad, Katherine Utley, Stephanie Schlabach, Jasmine Omidfar,
Cami Winding, Kelsey Ball, Savanna Frierson, America Garza, Taylor Kay, Michelle Lo,
Jamie Marvil, Emma Newbern, Somer Dice, Alexa Vizcano, Kate Pergler, Zelpha Williams
Allison Hinds, Melissa Vartanian, Katherine O'Donnell, Christine Urquhart, Eleni Venetos,
Lauren Closson, Jesslyn Whittell, Anna Behrens, Luisa de Carteret, Nell Zaloom, Cece Osborn,
Raika Dacquel, Angelica Maleski, Samantha Moriarty, Jordan Carfino, Zoe Otedola, Alexa Soto
Barbara Vliestra, Danielle Horton, Catherine Kidder, Janelle Lew, Nicole Chae, Kelly Cantrell,
Alison Tercero, Alex Marmureanu, Lauren Hall, Carly Klein, Blair Thompson, Meghan Murphy,
Jane Alt, Alex Baaden, Sommer Denison, Jenny Garabedian, Taylor Latimer, Genevieve Mazza,
Ali Griffiths, Rebecca Hextall, Katie Hathaway, Izzy Desantis, Kayla Dickie, Natalie Gigg,
Caroline & Julie Robinson, Candace, Kelsey Farrer, Jessie Mata, Megan Divine, Rose Lyn
Elizabeth & Alexandra Volpicelli, Zoe Daily,, Renee Meyer, Alison Park, Katrina Stevenson,
Cristina Alanis, Jacqueline Zachariadis, Mariana Aguilar, Bianca Bernal, Avery Bradshaw,
Danielle Burton, Megan Correnti, Caitlin Harris, (Mary Jo, Alex, Lea Madda), Milan Moore,
Julienne Nunn, Megan Percell, Ivana Rojas, Christine Soliman, Charity Watts, Maria Grosso
Beth Windler, Carly Zieminski, Joselyn Alvarado, Ashley Harris, Marie Hopkins, Helen Feng
Madison Kelleher, Katie Chalmers, Sara Hawley, Laurie Bathker, Kelsey Kays, Karen Nam,
Kelly O'kane, Chrsitine Barreda, Anjelica Garcia, Molly Lasater, Molly McGonigle
Lauren Nord, Evie Neptune, Renata Ooms, Alex Preston, Courtney & Casey Rea,
Allie Schwartz, Patricia Shatz, Jessica Smith, Katie Stennett, Hannah Tierney, Lauren Bergloff,
Virginia Anton, Tessa Boettcher, Jennifer Mainor, Maggie Notaro, Bonnie Ogilvie, Megan White
Cassie Hoppock, Elizabeth Tauro, Kristen Partipilo, Gizelle & Danielle Pera, Irina Popov,
Madison Wojciechowski, Abby Wollman, Alexia Rosenberg, Nicole Viole, Lauren Francois
Sara Rygiel, Margaret DiTullio, Alyssa Winthrop, Lea Mouallem, Jacqueline Schmitt, Kim Ali
Madison Akerblon, Brittan Hawken, Natasha Lederman, Mary Beth Marrone, Emily Mead
Taylor Carr, Alex Baraff, Sophie Shaeffer, Ruth Robbins, Hayley Selch, Maranda Henderson
Monica Cody, Tara Deadrick, Heather Dutton, Marrissa Masania, LaRie Burgoyne, Ellen Grasu
Julianna Castro, Tyra Causey, Christina Gordon, Claire Morris, Candace Coleman, Erin Huling
Lauren Hardgrove, Ashley McGinnis, Catherine Conkle, Kelly Curphey, Daniella Bermudez
Senna Chen, Teresa Lang, Melissa Tan, Brittany Mclaren, Brianna & Daira Silkaitis, Alex Fleder
Winta Stefanos, Christine Alcantar, Lauren Taylor, Lucy Galloway, Megan Riordan, Katie Billet
Brita Vinje, Hilary Feybush, Alix Fogel, Autum Gibbs, Isabella DiMarzio, Kelsey Gallagher
Lindsay Megan Mara Grumbo) Lisa Schmidt, Danielle Jimenez, Juliette Luini,
Cloudette Pattison, Brooke Pomerantz, Michelle Bellissimo Hayley Hindinger, Liz Legere,
Cheyenne Tucker, Chantelle La PortAra Jamasbi, Desiree Khoury, Bridget Kilroy,
Samantha Fowler, Marjorie PilovetzkyChristina Heinlein, Daine Reed, Jennifer Tan,
Gennea Squire, Christina Tabit, Torrie Takata Greer Tallant, Devan Randall, Amber Oleson,
Kathryn Perez, Erin Pearce, Carly Memsic Morgan MacCuish, Katie Holmes,
Kristen & Tyler Crothers, Kim, Alison, & Stephanie Alves, Alexandra Perazzelli, Lara Fareed
Emily Mazziotta, Karen Lotta, Camilla Ogeborn, Annya Lott, Nicole Diaco, Christina Dowling,
Jennifer Crowll, Elizabeth Cirelle, Kristen Kohl, Nicole Bush, Isabelle French, Katie Byrnes,
Natasha Srour, Shamin Rostami, Heather Foley, Kim Foster, Jennifer Kang Molly McRoskey,
Danielle Lauren Solis, Jennifer Battistello, Michelle Lefevre, Kayla Wilson
Kazanna Hames, Marika Decyk, Mayam Forghani, Lana & Sevan Petrosian, Laura Burgee
Katie Llewellyn, Katie Low, Julie Berman, Elizabeth Munson, Natalie Nelson, Kristen Cruise
Skye Ritvo, Daniel Steiner, Megan Hall, Erica Duke, Simone Harouche, Ksenia Chumakova
Jennifer Lacey, Arianna Schioldager, Jamie Nuwer, Noelle LE Blanc, Leila Tahmassebi
Whitney Engler, Emily Peacock, Melissa Solomon, Adrianna Ramogida, Birdie Bartholomew
Cassie Bryan, Natalie Bjelejac, Katherine Black, Amanda Bailey, Jennifer Bihr, Erica Sanborn
Dylan Blakely, Erin Everett, Caitlin Wilder, Beau Levinson, Emily Stabile, Cortney Kesselman
Dominique Abensour, Zachary Bainter, Kate Ball, Paul Baran, Kim Bathker, Marlene Bathker
Marina Benedict, Mary Benedict, Marilyn Bennett, Jill Bickett, Stephen Billington, Jim Bole
Margaret Brady, Amber Brown, Nicole Callahan, Michael Jones, Dave Clark, Herbert Campos
Ben Christensen, Dan Culbertson, Scott Crichlow, Kathy De Blois, Lindsay Delamontaigne
Cari Klein, Lyndsey DeMuro, Michelle DeVita, Teresa Dickey, Liz Driscoll, Valerie Dykeman
Judy Edwards, Marcy Enoch, Kevin Flinn, Rebecca Florido, Michelle Gergen, Janeatrie Gibson
Mary Elle Gozdecki, Tony Green, Rachel Grella-Harding, Claire Hackett, Sally Helin
David Herley, Vidal Hernandez, Cynthia Hoepner, Jennifer Hubbell, Erica Huebner, Emily Hull
Charles Hutchinson, Thomas Iannone, Kelli Huynk, Leslie Johnson, Marie Johnson, Chris Vivo
Lori Paillet, Natalie Paredes, Tia Johnson, Sylvia Jones, Robert Kelly, Bill Klein, Amie Kosberg
Jacqueline Landry, Amy Lebenzon, Tuan Le, Michelle Lee, Patrick E. Lynch, Patrick P. Lynch
Neil Talbot, Traci Maffei, Andria Marcus, Cindy Maresca, Alfredo Martinez, Margaret McKenna
Mary Ann McQueen, Theresa Menard, Ty Metcalfe, Debora Miller, Francisco Murillo
Fina Neubauer, Julianne O'Connor, Pamela Ocampo, Dellia Patino, Jae Perez, Steffany Perez
Jay Perini, Dina Petringa, Vinh Pham, Julia Phillips, Haley Powell, Aagie Ramos, Mary Resner
Sandy Smith, Elise Rodriguez, Erin Ruesler, Frances Ruth, Melissa Sakowski, Ronald Sampson
Jennifer Schassler, Deborah Scherer, Chris Schulte, Laura Holloway, Eddie Rossenberg
Fabrice Sene, Sydney Reece-Sene, Whitney Sholl, Nancy Spitz, Sharon Stephens, Sandy Uribe
Candace Savalas, John Stevens, Virginia Valenzuela, Julie Whittell, Tom Zimmerman

Table of Contents

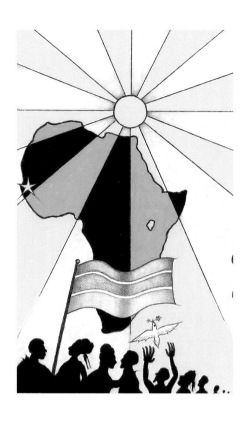

MY HERITAGE

My heritage does not belong to me.
It is never mine to own or sell,
However the windfalls of time may swing.
It will always be mine
To uphold, to celebrate, and to criticize.
It will always be mine
To contribute what I can master.
So that I can dangle in my blackness,
And I can slang in my African way,
To bring laughter and smiles to the children.
Sene-Gambia is where I sprang from,
So delightful a place.

I honor the people of the world for recognizing me,
For here I lay and for every second my heritage
Changes with every experience I gain.
There is Africa bold as day and raw as the fiery truth.
Can you hear the laughter, that is Africa.
There she goes all bold, bright, and beautiful.
Just makes me want to cry.

Scorpion publishing.com

PICK YOUR SIN

Please do not rush in like an end of year blowout sale
You can pick a very massive sin, then again
You can pick series of little sins
Best still, you can window shop all the sins.
I will not tell you which one is my favorite sin of all time
I am not allowed to give advice or give suggestions.
My job is to guide and explain to you the rules
Please do READ THE SMALL PRINT,
It is known to catch many smart folks.
Whatever you think, do, or dream I have it all,
Sinning is my business, and fun with suffering is my calling.
To sin in his name, no worries I can handle that
To sin in multiple ways and degrees,
no worries I can handle that
I can introduce you to many wonderful ways of sinning,
Prehistoric sinning, ancient sinning, iron age sinning,
And I also have some specials available.
If you are not sure, take all the time you need
No man on earth, or no woman alive will go without
Tasting my goodies.
Hope to see you soon
I am always ready and willing to serve
I will satisfy all your sinning needs and desires
If you don't call me, I will definitely be calling you.
Sinning is my business and fun with suffering is my game.

RABBIT'S FOOT

Why do rabbits reproduce so damn fast?
If people were not constantly after their feet
As a good luck charm,
Rabbits will take more of a romantic tone.
They will go out on more dates,
They will try teasing a little bit more,
They will have more time to know each other.
I guess you would be at it any chance you got
If they were chasing you for your lucky feet.
One never knows, does one?
When one is to loose one's feet... does one?
Rabbit stew I don't mind.
But just for one's so-called lucky feet
If they were so lucky,
Look how much of a lucky charm they are to me
And I have all four of them.
I wish I had three lives
Unlike some who manage to have nine lives
With all their feet intact.

Scorpion publishing.com

MAYA ANGELOU

You, the sister to the beautiful ones
You, the charmer to the wiser ones
You the sister,
You the mother,
You the grandmother,
To one and all black people.
You a true witness to our testy life.
Oh my goodness, the devilish sweetness
You bring to the written word.
In your presence you stab, jab, twist, and rinse
The spoken word.
To gingerly shake... and shake... and shake
The truth in all.
In all of us.
Your joyous humor and fun,
You kindly swing... and swing... and swing
To the rhythm of the sunlight,
For your open deliciousness enlightens the spirits
And arouses the soul to perfection.
Then you timely walk away with our ears,
And minds waiting
For more, more of your cultured sweetness.

THE RIVER GAMBIA

Who are you?
A River!
A sweet water river
Who are you?
A River!
But you speak the language of the old,
And you know the laws that have passed.
Who are you?
A River!
But you tell the stories of tomorrow,
And redefine your shape as you please
Who are you?
A River!
But you feel the pain of your troubled children,
And you know their aching spirits.
Who are you?
A River!
But the wisdom you seek is beyond the present,
And you heal, feed, and give joy,
You love, hurt, and give birth.
Grieve at times..., sudden grief.
Who are you?
A River! I am a river.
Must I be human too?
I am a River for all ages.
I am a River!

DISREGARD MY WEALTH

My wife definitely loves my so-called humor.
My son, my hero,
My daughter, my heroine,
My brother, my pity,
My sister, my happiness,
My father, my honor,
My mother, my honor,
My neighbor, my friend,
My friend, my liar,
My driver, (whisperingly) my right hand man,
My doctor, my future,
My lawyer, my money,
My lady mistress my money.

SPARKLE

Tricks of the trade
Or tricks to trade
The unwanted stuff
We are so inclined to buy
The useless stuff
We all so gather and comply
Things that stood collecting dust
Collecting insects we all so despise
Things we stumble over
Things we knock over
Things we fight over
Things we think we cannot do without
The truth is
There is nothing
Absolutely nothing
We can't do without.
The tricks to trade things by us
The great tricks that the mind plays on us
The best deals or the worst deals
All of us do like a good deal
Deal me the trick to use on my next trade.
Here is a deal that is a trick for a life time.
A must buy: Buy a gushing wind
to help your ship sail fastest.

TO THE SOUL ABOVE

I want you to hear me,
I want you to hear me love you,
With your eyes...
With your ears...
With your heart...
With your eternal soul...
Hear me love you...
I want you to hear me,
I want you to hear me,
Love you,
Between my every thought...
Between my every laughter...
Between my every Heart-filled breath of your scent...
Hear me love you.
I want you to hear me,
I want you to hear me,
Love you
Sincerely with every imperial love instilled in me.
Hear me love you.

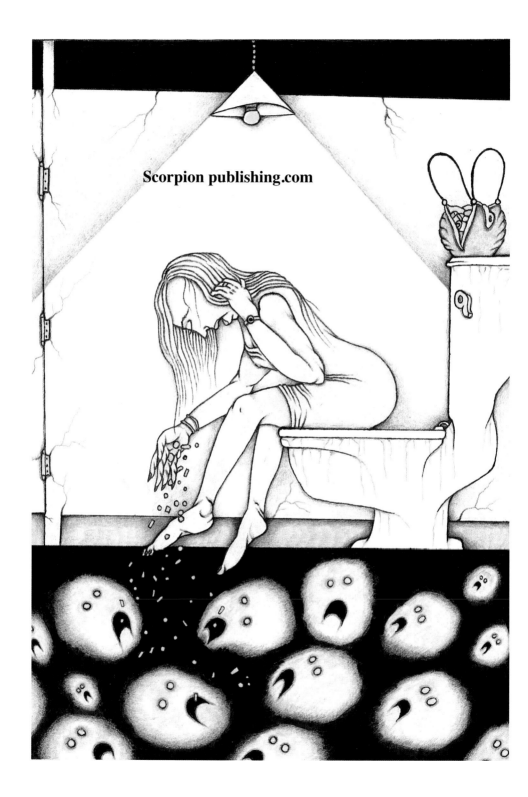

MY NAME IS COCAINE

Beware, my friend, my name is Cocaine,
Coke for short, or the rock.
I entered this country without a passport.
Ever since then I've been hunted and sought.
I'm more valued than diamonds, more treasured than gold,
Use me just once and you too will be sold.
I'll make a schoolboy forget his books,
I'll make a beauty queen neglect her looks,
I'll take a renowned speaker and make him a bore,
I'll take your mamma and make her a whore,
I'll make a schoolteacher forget how to teach,
I'll make a preacher not want to preach.
All kinds of people have fallen under my wing!
Look around! See the results of my sting.
I've got daughters turning on their mothers,
I've got brothers robbing their sisters,
I've got burglars robbing the Lord's house,
I've got husbands pimping their spouse.
I'm the king of crime and the price of destruction,
I'll make your body organs malfunction,
I'll cause your babies to be born hooked,
I'll turn the most honest of men into crooks,
I'll make you rob, steal, and kill,
When you're under my power, you'll have no will.
Well, now you know. What will you do?
Remember, my friend, it's all up to you.
If you decide to jump in my saddle,
You better ride me well,
For on the white horse of Cocaine,
I'll ride you straight to hell.

A CHILD'S GOD

God made the heavens
God made the earth
God made man
Who made God?

I know! I know!
Put your hand down young Karim
I know who made God.
Come now put your hand down, the father
Does not have time for our shenanigans today.

Now... now... don't be upset,
Please do not cry.
Alright let him answer
Go ahead, who made God?

Oh I am dying to hear this, father,
You took the words right out of my mouth.
My mother!
Did you say your mother...?
It's a miracle
God bless your dear mother
With a mouth like yours
Even my praying for you will not help her.

ANCIENT TIMES

Chasing the forbidden fruit
It always looks bigger, brighter, and sweeter
Every time you see, hear, touch, smell,
Or think about it
It pokes its desirability in your daily existence
With a daring stare at your crafty curiosity
Knowing the shocking consequence,
but the temptation is much greater.
Are you being tested or triple dared?
How badly do you want it?
Isn't it to die for?
It must be the answer to all your riddles.
All those who love you will tell you not to do it?
Less than a handful will tell you to go for it.
It has the devil's handwritings on it.
Then again, what can the devil do to a big strong,
And clever person like you?
Remember you are invincible.

TOAD

If a princess kisses a toad
It will turn into a handsome prince.
Ah... that's what I call old fashion birth control
Princesses go around kissing toads
That will never turn into princes
I know,
I was once a prince
But toads get all the kisses,
I became a toad
If you can't beat them, join them
Now that I am a toad
Kissing toads is no longer fashionable
What a charmed life
I have...
If you can't beat them, wait your turn
Maybe if you wait long enough
Kissing toads will become fashionable again.
If only I stayed being a prince
One day a princess will feel pity for you
It beats being a toad.

YEAH! MY WITNESS

One needs to grow,
One must do so childishly.
One needs to learn,
One must do so progressively fast.
One needs to love,
One must do so with compassion for others.
One needs to forgive,
One must do so with a hug.
One needs to cry,
One must do so to forget the past and welcome
A new era.
One needs to change,
One must do so to taste what you are missing.

MY CLOSEST FRIENDS

Once, twice, thrice,
Suddenly a friend of a friend knocked on my door.
Once, twice, thrice,
I jumped off the bed, half dazed but quick enough
To open the door to a friend of a friend.
Once, twice, thrice,
A friend of a friend broke the news to me calmly
That a willing friend of a friend wants me to visit.
Once, twice, thrice,
A friend of a friend I visited met numerous
Friends of accepted friends.
We joked, laughed, sang, danced,
Some drank, and the rest smoked.
Good byes were said, hugs, and kisses, here
And there and all over.
Some promises were made, for what they were worth.
Some walked, some ran, some rode, some drove,
And some flew away home.
Some became addicts
Some became idealists
Some succeeded in a man's world
Some disappeared and some reappeared
Some were ever present.
Finally, in dust we all met.

FLAIR

The things we know are rich
The things we don't know reign
Creativity with a sassy touch
Brightness flows while the spirit lures with signals of torch.
The unknown dangling with a teasing frame
Knowing the rules helps to win the game.
Qualifying with the required characteristics will help
I wonder what they are?
To be a voted member feels just a little special
But to be a needed friend in desperate times is more special
To wear that jacket of honor,
With that perfect color.
That says to everyone I got the right stuff.
To say I belong.
To what...?
To the best there is
To the best there will ever be.
You are only the best in your era.
That is the best way to dress up in any era.

TRUTH OR DARE

River of molten gold flowing away
Some by nature's deeds
Some by man's greed
We are all wishing to fulfill our needs
The farmer's crops or the cities lawns
The wailing drought we've known about for centuries
Is no doubt creeping closer for us to bare it all?
When the scam ends
Who will pay the dividends?
These woven blankets need fairly
Compromising hearts to lead.
Drought... drought ... Drought
They will scream
Who cares about the price of gas?
We need more tearful flowing prayers
I thought we already tried that.
The naked rain dance could be a new trend in California
Vanishing lawns or over priced healthy crops
Water!
Is too precious to waste
This bucket is not going away in haste.

Scorpion publishing.com

I AM A M-A-N

If I were a bird
I'd fly,
I'd fly,
And I'd fly so high in the blue sky
So that no ill faith of man will come to me.

If I were a fish
I'd swim,
I'd swim,
And I'd swim so deep in the blue Ocean
So that no ill faith of man will come to me

If I were an animal
I'd run
I'd run
And I'd run so fast in the thick dark forest
So that no ill faith of man will come to me

I am not a bird
I am not a fish
I am not an animal
I am only a M-A-N

I wish no ill faith of man would come to me.

I AM SOLD

When you are buying shoes
Please make sure you take your feet with you.
For buying shoes by sight
Will cause you surprising pain
Just like red ants in your pants.
The only thing about shoes is, they are on your feet
For as long as you are willing to bear the pain or as long
As you are willing to hide your embarrassing feet.
I will prefer to hide my embarrassing feet.
When you are buying knickers
Please do not be embarrassed
Just imagine you are a Victoria's Secret's super model
When it comes down to it
In one time or another
We are all someone's Victoria's Secret super model.
Even if it was in passing.
Be as bold as lightening
And let your hair down and enjoy
All the pleasures that are ahead of you.

WAY OUT

If one has a choice
Not barring fate or destiny
Which way will you go?
Will you go with a bang?
Or will you go quietly?
Considering all my choices
I guess the best thing to do is to wait
Considering all my choices,
I will wait till I am surprised
On the very day and the very method
It's best for it to be a sudden surprise.
Do not be sucked,
It is time to checkout anyway
Before I begin to be sound like an old conservative.

WOMAN

You got it
You got it all
Just be yourself
Keep them guessing
Never walk too slowly
Never walk too fast
Just walk it ...
Do not ask, just demand chocolates
Lots of chocolates... it's good for the inner spirit
Go ahead... gossip
It's OK To gossip all you want it's good therapy for free
Take your time
Do not rush
"But I am going to be late," you think
Let them wait! A queen must always be waited upon
Oh yes... be a little bit jealous,
It improves the circulation
At times be mean spirited...
It will keep everyone on their toes
Be bitchy...
Even God loves a little bitchy.
Bitch as much you like
But do not ever whine

Whining takes the taste off a good meal
Be bold and speak your mind ...
At all times but not at funeral
Oh you can change your mind as many times,
As many different colors that seem to catch your eyes
Be difficult ... Be very difficult ...
You will always be remembered.
Please do not let anyone call you "BABY"
It's just too elementary
Woman it's your world
Live it sister... taste it all
You deserve the best
Nothing less than the very best
Enjoy it
Enjoy it all
More power to you
Please do not ever let men understand you.
That's the way it should be.

Scorpion publishing.com

THIS IS THE MAN I KNOW

This is the man I know,
The man I know is standing in front of me
With an incorruptible jolly wide smile at all times.
This is the man I don't know,
The man I don't know is the man who hurriedly hits
The bar, pubs and clubs in the shadow of darkness,
Heavily begging to drown his will.
This is the man I don't know,
The man I don't know is the man who can get any
Executive job if he wants after four months if
They are lucky. He will easily throw it away for the abuse.
With a bag full of excuses for this that and everything
This is the man I know,
The man I know is always gentle, caring and shows
Real affection towards all creatures. He is likeable,
Loving and charming even at the worst of times.
This is the man I know,
The man I don't know is the man sadly we don't want
To see, hear, or talk about. Sorry, that's why each and
Every one of us has to work a lot harder to make this world
A better place.
This is the man I know,
The man I know I truly believe in, deep down inside,
Each and every one of us there is the man I know.

GRACE

For unknown reason
You sneak into my every thought,
My every reasoning,
My every imagination,
My every fantasy.
As the sunlight peak into the dawn
I wonder why you of all people
Are not even a formidable enemy?
Pardon me,
I am going to be as honest as
a straight right punch on the nose.
I am head over heels in love
You are like a warm blanket of pleasure
Healing my every weakness.
Of course it is a natural human mistake,
To fall in love
And have it written all over your face.
Lie you may, but this secret cannot be wiped off
Just like tears of joy or sorrow.
Love is the invisible Godlike hand that tickles
The uniqueness to aspire.
The hidden courage to open ???

ONE OUT OF A BILLION

Man is born with nothing,
Man dies with nothing,
Yet man lives to get everything.
I live with your smile,
I sleep and wake up in your scent,
May I have the chance to forever blossom?
My life with your daily distractions,
I may have lost the chance to be the richest
Man in the world,
I may have forever quelled my love of sports,
But I hope one day before I die
I can say to my mother,
You are nothing like mother.
She is trying hard to like you
And you are pretending to like her
Together the house is raging hot.
It's only my opinion.

WHY DID THE CHICKEN CROSS THE ROAD?

Why did the chicken cross the road?
I do not know, why did the chicken cross the road?
To get to the other side.

One summer's day I saw a chicken crossing the road
I asked the chicken "why are you crossing the road?"
The chicken stared at me with a puzzled look and then said,
"I plead the fifth, then again, that is none of your business.
How dare you ask me why I am crossing the road?
I have two feet, and two eyes like everyone else
I can cross the road like everyone else,
Whenever I feel like it.
"What nerve!
If you really want to know.
I will plead the fifth."

Ah! That must be an American chicken
Even chickens know their rights in America,
And they are not afraid to express their freedom of speech.
I guess this chicken will not be for dinner tonight.
Just imagine if chickens could vote?

FAIR IS FAIR

Tap your feet
Clap your hands
Sway side to side
Raise your voice and sing out loud
The guns they carry will never be used on you
The machetes they are carrying will never be used on you
The teargas canisters will never be used
To displace your rightful protest
Tap your feet
Clap your hands
Sway side to side
Raise your voice and sing out loud
We embrace a democratic system of politics now
But after every election
One side always cries foul
The elections were floored
They were neither free nor fair
You can swallow the over-the-top negative rhetoric
But the outcome of elections always ends up being
Senseless killings,
Streams of blood
Streams of tears.
If grown ups cannot act like grown ups
Why don't we let the children vote?
At least we know it's their future
Even if they elect the wrong people
Most of these people we are dying to elect
Can't even win an argument in their own household.

MY LOS ANGELES

L.A., a name state of mind. Stylist to the image of kind.
Letterheads concede a glimpse of indifference,
Colorful commotion of subjective tolerance.
Expect the eternity of creativity,
Explore the rhythmic cultures of peace
Looking from a distance to retreat.
The everlasting fortune upholds a treat
Stirring down The mighty in politicized mode,
Bearing all its dislikes in digital code.
Apprehending of the hissing voices of universal cure
Need it not hope, but arrogance of trust to endure
Starlight with random rays choose the next victim.
For the media beast
A little romantic dinner on every third Monday.

Rolling side to side with either breast a star is born,
Or just a star is made for the media beast to chew on.
Yet the order side wakes up in tears,
With death circling and gunshots echoing
Occasionally the chosen give to the damned.
L.A. is kind, gentle, loving at times
The sky kisses us with hopeful movies to enjoy.
Our education is fruitfully flourishing at all corners,
We are strong together,
When a child that used to sit at the corner
With hope is given inspiration by a movie,
To grow up and fulfill that dream with angels
On either side and help us carry L. A. higher and higher
closer to the heavens.
With a movie to inspire the next child.

A WISH

If I knew the contents of your intentions,
I'd be ready to fight for your innocence.
Have you ever heard the cry of a chick eagle?
It says, "I wish I could fly, I'll get all the food
I want." It's tired of waiting to be fed.

I wish I could fly,
I wish I could fly,
I wish I could fly.

But the day the chick eagle flew, it flew far and wide,
For days and nights, without food.
The eagle wished it could never fly.
For it was not taught how to be a better hunter.
Be VERY SPECIFIC with what you wish for,
If not there can be bitter surprises waiting for you.
Please, child, wait till you're capable of paying
Your way before you can talk back to your parents.
At least wait till you are out of the house.

SHE WANTS ME...

She wants me to be jealous
She wants me to be bossy
She wants me to be nice and kind
She wants me to be generous
She wants me to open doors for her
She wants me to be ghetto at times
She wants me to be sophisticated at times
She wants me to be strong and fearless
She wants me to be "Mr. Know-it-all"
But she will not hesitate to put me in my place.
She wants me to love her more every second
She wants me... she wants me to surprise her with gifts
Say that's all right with me.
As far as I am myself
When I am around my friends and especially mama.
I must be confusing you
She wants to be my fashion designer
She wants to make me only her man
She just wants to be my doctor, lawyer, accountant, teacher,
Chef, adviser, lover, and friend,
I do not want her to be my mother.
And she wants to be my everything...!

TO ANY BLACK CHILD

Education...!

Education...!

Education...!

You open their eyes to see differently,
You open their minds to think differently
You open their hearts to love differently,
You speak to them close to feel differently,
You teach them to know differently.
For centuries we harassed, insulted, enslaved, and murdered
For generations we left with nothing gained,
Nowadays we may be tolerated,
But when will we be accepted?
I hope that we are not what we are forever,
I hope we are not how we are forever.
We can contribute to what we can be forever.

TAKE A BOW

The joy you seek
The blessing you seek
The love you seek
The wealth you seek
The health you seek
The knowledge and wisdom you seek,

Will take you far away from home
Will make you cry till you are tearless
Will force you to swallow your pride a few more times
Than you can count
Will make you compromise and associate
With personal non-credo
Will often times lead you to a world of sin.

Yet if you're strong enough
Stubborn enough
Cunning enough
Smart enough
Patient enough
Disciplined enough

Lastly if you believe in hard-work
And not to listen to
All the lies people shower you with,
You will come out on top.
Without losing many friends.

TILL LIES DO US APART

His roaming eyes,
Made her curious about his lies.
Naturally, her thick forest shooting vibes
Made him assassinate her with his slick fibs.
Add ten years of spying,
And five years of crying
Her welcomed busy life earned a gold heart.
His lonely nightmare to father all,
Earned him an artificial heart.
Each had been blessed,
Sometimes with instant prayer,
Or most times with lasting, one lasting prayer.

I SHALL NOT BE DENIED

You think of him.
You can only wonder
Yes, none came better prepared.
Stronger, wiser, kinder and greatness he stood for.
Who else?
The only man who eats his daily meals on God's table.
I struggle to find the right words,
None of the words in all the languages in the world
Could truly express his might.
A freedom fighter that had people dancing with rage
27 years as a prisoner with NO MALICE.
Yet he is as humble as a goodnight kiss.
You may ask what were they afraid of?
To reborn this Rainbow Nation of love for all to admire.
A leader to measure all presidents
Just by name he is an inspiration to end all petty angers.
He has the COURAGE
TO SAY NO MORE
TO LEAD FROM THE FRONT
NOT TO EMBARRASS ANYONE
TO SHARE WITH ALL HE HAS
TO CARE WITH ALL HIS MIGHT
TO LOVE WITH ALL HIS HEART
NELSON MANDELA.
My father's only hero since the 60s.
Little did I know
NELSON MANDELA will surpass all my superheroes.

NUMBERS

1 2 3...
3 is so happy it is accompanied by 1& 2
But extremely worried about 4
3 just cannot get hold of 4

4 5 6...
6 is so worried about half past 6 and 7
7 is such an appointment time
All dates want to meet at 7

7 8 9....
7 loves 8
Because 8 is also cool and calm
But 9 is always a rude number
Almost nobody makes it at 9

10 11 12....
10 is open for anything
While 11 can never say no to 12
Be aware of 12
12 makes everyone begin to dream of the
End of the day or night life is just beginning.
The witching hour arrives dreamily at 12 midnight.
Be ready to mess around.

SUN- LOVING RASCAL

Hey...! Hey...!
What type of smile are you wearing
Today?
Friend, my best friend,
I smile at the sun-loving rascal like you.
When I saw that smile,
Such a sweet good-time smile,
I knew it was real, all real.
So real a genuine smile that I understood
Our love can never stop growing.
The bad news is in our hearts there are real genuine
Smiles that will always enrich our love.

CONTROL SPEED

Many people die of it
Many more people will die of it.
No matter how loud we scream
Slow down... slow down...
Many people will speed to kill.
Reckless or a taste for freedom
The speed, yes faster and faster
Speed we all yearn for.
Car, bike, train, plane, boat, or on feet
Speed... who is faster, which is faster?
Am I the quickest?
Am I the fastest?
It's only an ego or expression of divinity,
But to die of it.
Must be the dumbest way to go.
To kill others must be the worst way to live..
Controlled speed is the best way to approach life
At all times. Safety first, safety second,
Safety always and safety forever.
Slow down... slow down for all...
All will be safer.
All will be safer in our beds.
There is no need to lose this one sweet life
Nor is it honorable to take a life.

EARTHQUAKE

I was told we have earthquakes here
My face beamed a delightful smile
I am deadly serious she barked on for me to hear
In my virgin mind
I am basking in the scent of wealth and movie star smiles
I felt a tremendous grab of my legs
My legs, my never failing legs
There was a single jolt and a brave warming pause
The earth began a very ancient dance as old as creation
Yet as young as our mere tomorrow
I was here before you
Where do you think the avalanche got its name?
How about the whirlwind's circling toil
Ah fire! Fire's raging flame
Just like Mohammed Ali introduced rap, invented
Trash Talking, and gave us showboating
To a higher epsilon of advertising
Yet any young hungry cat tries to be the creator
I was the first so I shall teach you a little thing about
Shaking and dancing.

BYE BOYS

Hold it... hold it...
A smile for all ages
Peaceful yet sweetly full of cunning youth
Happy yet chilled full of surprises
A star rising with her every kissing hope
Tingling wanting of each fulfilling breath
Most beautiful spread to humble all heaven
Love or live...
Oh corrupt me
Oh corrupt me much more
So much that in each breath
All shall be about you.
So I dream the more pleasurable skin-to-skin dance
So I curse each slip of a tongue that ends with your name
My star is nailed to a crossroad waiting on you.
For God sakes I am screaming
For a twitch... Twitch...
Muscles ache like never for a piece
Twitch... twitch... Twitch...
My heart cries for you.
My soul is yearning for you.
Twitch... twitch... Twitch...
Give us a kiss that will take me an extra mile.

IT IS OKAY TO CRY

The worried child
There are the worried parents.
Scared to death to speak up for their child,
It has to be... NO! It must be the tradition that can
Only handcuff parents this way.
Where are the worried friends?
They all say the child has
The devil living in her.
The devil living in him.
Where are the champions for our children?
Who are you crying for, child?
Are you waiting for the devil to come and save you?
The child is crying for those children
That were MURDERED because the old woman
Said, "There is a devil living in that child"
Why should the devil want to live in a child?
If you were the devil would you want to live in a child?
Or would you want to live in people with the influence?
Surely the devil will not pick a weak, sickly, meager, and
Afraid child to show its might.
To further the devil's agenda like an express virus.
If I were the Devil I would prefer to live
Within the rich and famous,
So that I can have great influence.
We happily watch our children being taking advantage of.
How brutally wicked such a phrase can bury a child.
It is tough to be a child.
Shame on you, Shame on us all.

KILLER HONEY

This is a stick up!
This is a stick up!
I saw no gun in her hands, nor a weapon.
She just walked by me. Real slow.
Her every chosen step rocks the soul of my being,
And leaves my mind screaming.

This is a stick up!
This is a stick up!
For her sweet being outshines the Sun,
For at this point and time her enchanting grace compliments
The fairest of all the heavenly angels.

This is a stick up!
This is a stick up!
Continued to ring in my lust drunk mind
I see no further than her illuminating beauty
That glows a billion times brighter than the Moon.

This is a stick up
This is a stick up
What a killer honey?
I do want every piece of that killer honey
That killer honey
That killer honey.

IT IS A SMALL WORLD

One day our paths will cross again
It is a small world
When you have your canvas ready
With brush set ready
To create your masterpiece of life
There is a small chance
I will be selling you your paint
It is a small world
I will not sell you the bright red paint you seek
But with the right offer, I will throw in the sky blue
And purple in for free.
It is a small world
Be careful the toes you step on when you are climbing
Your way up the ladder to the top.
Someday when you are coming down
We will be waiting with golden mallets to make sure
You pay for the pain you cause us forgotten nobodies.
It is a small world
Don't you ever forget it.

SNAP... SNAP... SNAP ...

It is raining tears of joy
It is raining tears of sorrow
It is just raining to our joy
It is just raining to save our sorrow

Snap... snap... Snap...
Where are the rain dancers?
Are they rejoicing or are they moving to the next dry place?
I bet they do not like the rain.
It must be their excuse to practice their new songs and
dance.

Snap... snap... Snap...
I wish one could snap their fingers to make it rain
When it rains just enough everybody is happy.
Snap... snap... Snap...
To make rain one will snap their fingers again.

If it rains too little no one is happy.
If it just rains too much no one will be happy.

SLEEP IN NO FEAR

The Angels of Sleep will visit everybody
One or more times in any hour of day or night
We shall be called upon, each and every one of us,
By the particular times of our body clocks,
To sleep in no fear.
The Angels of Sleep make sure we pay
The equivalent amount of hours and days,
We go without our body sleep.
We shall sleep in no fear,
In parks, airports, trains, cars, ship, at times
Even in toilets, on desks in schools or at work,
Occasionally in open fields, standing up, leaning on somebody,
and yet most of us prefer beds with all this,
We sleep in no fear.
The Angels of Sleep take pride to make sure we sleep
Anywhere, at anytime or in any season,
We sleep in no fear.
Thou shall sleep joyfully, comfortably, dreamily,
Or even sickly.
Our loved ones watch over us in peace,
Occasionally photos are taken
And blankets are placed over us,
Our enemies would surprise attack us,
But we sleep in no fear.
When the Angels of Sleep leave,
Some wake up where they left off,
Some in oceans of wealth,
Or tainted horror.
While some will sleep into the graves of hell or heaven.
To my amazement, we still sleep in no fear.

SIMPLE-MINDED

I looked back for what I could see.
I looked back trying to hear the words you spoke
In my defense.

If you did not tell and we were neither seen nor heard,
How could he have known?
Not a soul could have heard my serenading heart
Aching for you,
For your sweetly driven passion.

I saw you as a diverging light, which seemed to brighten,
To brighten my discharged soul into the extreme
Depths of jazz and blues.
For now and forever I will forgive your simple-minded.

STANDING AWAY

Upping out to stand alone,
Upping out to stay without food,
Upping out not to prove my maturity,
Nor my masculinity, but a slim linkage
Of rich and poor.
Shall I continue with the self-torturing?
Shall I keep struggling for my faith?
Shall I surrender my individual freedom of choice?
As tradition to live without fame or beauty,
But near the end of seeing the social status
Of the recycled community drop flat to a
Level of hatred between us?

I HEARD

The picture is perfect now
For mother to see
The story is clean enough now
For the children to read
The money is high enough now
For me to tell it all
My side, their side, and a little bit more money
I will even tell your side of the story
Everything that you heard that was off the record
Is now on the record
I have no more pain now
I only have to tell the truth for the devil to set me free.
I wonder how many more ways can the truth be told?
By the eyes, ears, mouth, nose, and skin.
What's in it for me?

PASSER – BY, THANK YOU

As a rich man
I can live the life of a rich man,
And I can die like a rich man.
As a middle class man
I can live the life of the middle class,
And I hope I know the place before I die.
As a poor man
I can live the life of a poor man,
And I can die like a poor man.

As rich man,
When I die
Everybody knows that I am dead.
I am dressed expensively,
Decorated in gold and diamond chains,
To my funeral a fleet of imported cars
Will cause traffic jams for hours,
My wealth is shared
With my family, the state or my next of kin,
Who fight for every last coin I had,
The ones I hate most are the ones
Who pretend to know me?
As for the middle class,
When I die
The ones who come
Are my very close friends?
A mixture of rich, middle and poor
My wealth – if I have any –
Is mostly shared amongst the ones I owed.
As a poor man
Only the six-foot ditch
Knows I am dead,
Wrapped in a kind of rage
With the handful of passers-by present.
If I happen to say a little prayer before my death,
I will have been glad to be born in the first place,
Made my life the best I could
But died with a lot of laughs.

KID

I know you are just trying to figure things out
But why are you in such a hurry to grow up?
I love your confidence and your passion?
I love the way you care so much?
I do not want you to rush and become an adult,
Because once you become an adult,
There is no going back.
I want you to have lots of fun things
To remember about your childhood.
Try to hold on to your childhood
Like those old superstar has-beens that refused to retire.
They are ready to play as long as they can lace their shoes,
They hang on till they're swept up with the trash.
Try everything at least once.
Read everything you can lay your hands on.
Do not stop yourself from trying something
Before you make up your mind "I do not like it"
Hang on to your childhood for dear life
Do not get bribed or bamboozled about being an adult.
It is really tough ...!
It is really a tough world out there...!
Be smart. Stay in school as long as possible,
Go get yourself as many degrees as possible.
Be your own BOSS.

MARYMOUNT HIGH SCHOOL

This small sensational place on Sunset
Is the place where miracles happen everyday
And we call them blessings.
Where all the people of the world meet
And all the languages of the world are shared.
Where girls come to, and leave as young women
With sophistication, originality, and strength of love
To change the world.
It's a place where the individual merits are celebrated
Fashion, movies, and music are expressed in joyful passing
Where handshakes are acceptable but hugs are the norm
Yes, it's true... Yes, it's very true...
It's a place where all the difficult questions are answered
With great emphasis on free speech.
Sports is an integral lifeblood of our daily pursuit of perfection,
Where we are known to compete like sailors.
To Fight..! Fight..! Fight...! GO SAILORS!
At day's end, we go back to toil with our never ending homework
Till the wee hours of the morning.
And some teachers act surprised when we sleep in class.
Marymount... Marymount... Marymount...
Is where the halo of goodness continues and
Victories of all our prayers are answered.
Where all the students are smarter than their parents
They are always in the forefront of social change and greatly
Involved in all aspects of charitable programs.
Where all the teachers are stylists, and are geniuses
They are known to grade fairly but firm.
Where all the parents are supportive, and delightful
With all the multitudes of joyous hope they have to endure.
How rare and unique we the blessed come together to change.

About the author

Lasan Seni Darboe was born in The Gambia, West Africa.
He lived in Fajara, and attended Gambia High School.
As a young poet he lived in London, England before
Relocating to Los Angeles, California.
In college he studied Business Administration
And Fitness & Nutrition.
Currently Mr. Darboe splits his time between
Writing poetry and children's books and coaching
Youth sports in West Los Angeles, for
Marymount High School,
Galaxy Alliance Soccer Club,
HI-Speed Track Club.

Other books published by Lasan Seni Darboe

True Colors Of The Chameleon 2007
My Name Is Cocaine And Other Poems 2001